Hello, Family Members,

Learning to read is one of the most important accomplishments of early childhood. **Hello Reader!** books are designed to help children become skilled readers who like to read. Beginning readers learn to read by remembering frequently used words like "the," "is," and "and"; by using phonics skills to decode new words; and by interpreting picture and text clues. These books provide both the stories children enjoy and the structure they need to read fluently and independently. Here are suggestions for helping your child *before*, *during*, and *after* reading:

Before

- Look at the cover and pictures and have your child predict what the story is about.
- Read the story to your child.
- Encourage your child to chime in with familiar words and phrases.
- Echo read with your child by reading a line first and having your child read it after you do.

During

- Have your child think about a word he or she does not recognize right away. Provide hints such as "Let's see if we know the sounds" and "Have we read other words like this one?"
- Encourage your child to use phonics skills to sound out new words.
- Provide the word for your child when more assistance is needed so that he or she does not struggle and the experience of reading with you is a positive one.
- Encourage your child to have fun by reading with a lot of expression . . . like an actor!

After

- Have your child keep lists of interesting and favorite words.
- Encourage your child to read the books over and over again. Have him or her read to brothers, sisters, grandparents, and even teddy bears. Repeated readings develop confidence in young readers.
- Talk about the stories. Ask and answer questions. Share ideas about the funniest and most interesting characters and events in the stories.

I do hope that you and your child enjoy this book.

> — Francie Alexander
> Chief Education Officer,
> Scholastic's Learning Ventures

For Jeremiah Merritt
— C.N.

For my aunt, Frances Harris, who nurtured my
love of art and painting and for my grandfather, Irwin Horlbeck,
who gave me his support and his love of the ocean
— G.H.

With thanks to Dr. Marcelo Carvalho
of the American Museum of Natural History

Go to scholastic.com for web site information on
Scholastic authors and illustrators.

Library of Congress Cataloging-in-Publication Data

Nichols, Catherine.
    Sharks! / by Catherine Nichols; illustrated by Greg Harris.
    p. cm. – (Hello reader! Science–Level 1)
    "Cartwheel books."
    Summary: An easy-to-read introduction to sharks and their physical characteristics
and eating habits.
    ISBN 0-439-32096-8 (pbk.)
    1. Sharks—Juvenile literature. [1. Sharks.] I. Harris, Greg, ill. II. Title. III. Hello
science reader! Level 1.

    QL638.9 .N49 2002
    597.3–dc21

                                                                        2001049036

10 9 8 7 6

                                                                    03 04 05 06
                    Printed in the U.S.A.
                    First printing, April 2002

by Catherine Nichols
Illustrated by Greg Harris

Hello Reader! Science — Level 1

SCHOLASTIC INC.

New York   Toronto   London   Auckland   Sydney
Mexico City   New Delhi   Hong Kong   Buenos Aires

Out in the ocean,
something is swimming.
What is it?

It's a shark!

A shark is a fish.

There are many, many kinds
of sharks.
Some are so small that they
can fit in your hand.

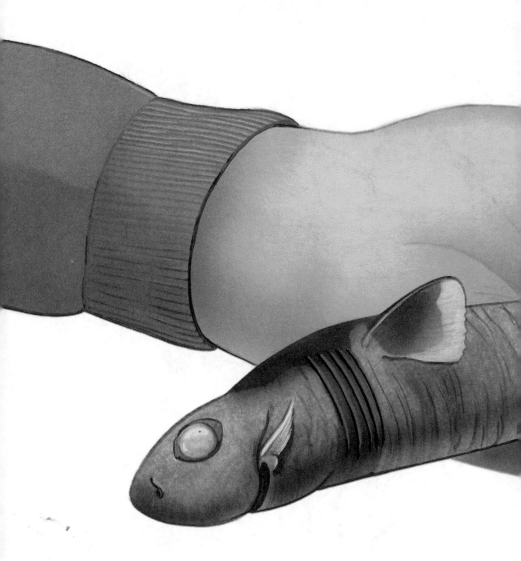

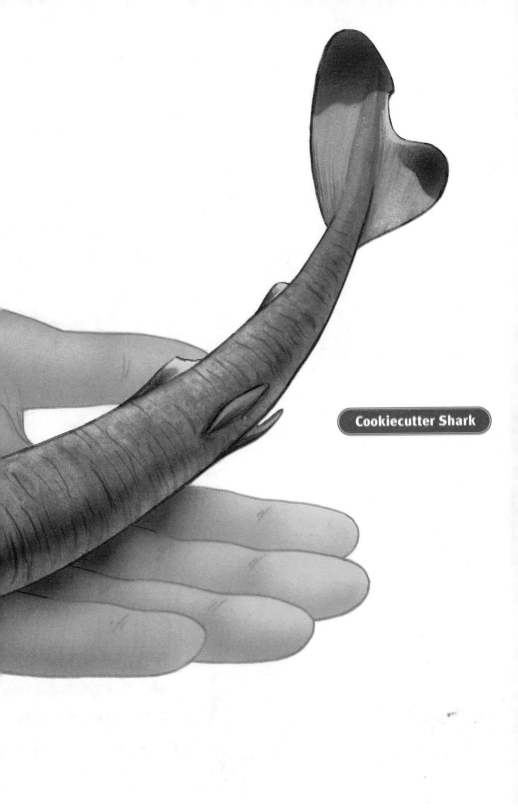

Cookiecutter Shark

Others are bigger than
a school bus!

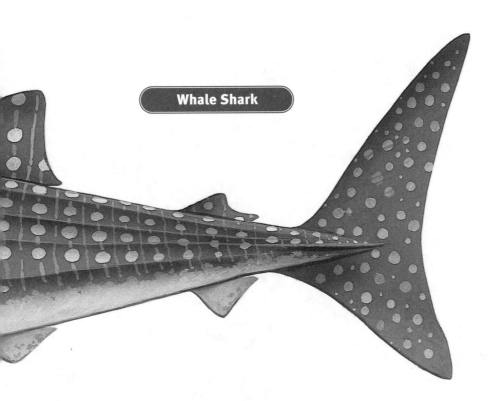

Whale Shark

Spinner Sharks

Most sharks have long,
rounded bodies.

Not this shark!
Its body is as flat as a pancake.

Angel Shark

These sharks' heads are shaped like hammers.

Hammerhead Sharks

A shark's snout can be long
and pointed . . .

Sawshark

Catshark

or short and wide.

Each shark has a tail that helps it swim.

Nurse Shark

Zebra Shark

Mako Shark

This shark has a long and
powerful tail.

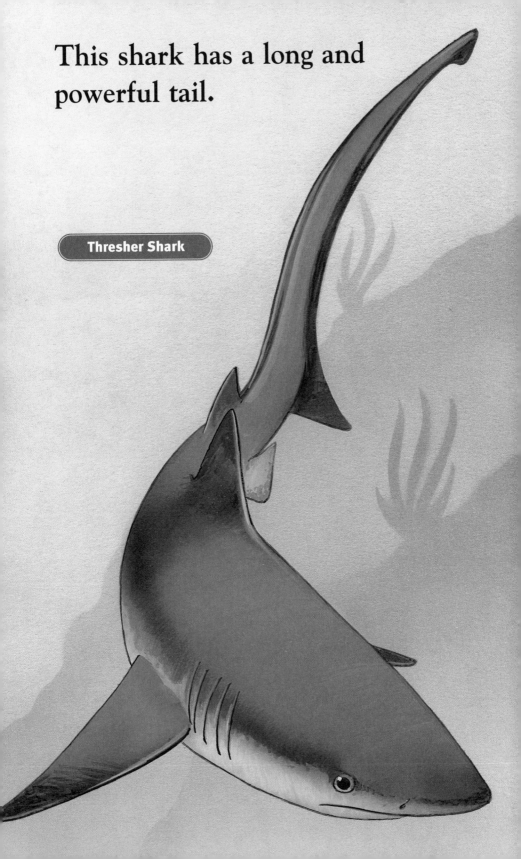

Thresher Shark

These sharks have strong jaws
and sharp teeth.
They are the sharks that people
fear the most.

This shark may also be dangerous.
It eats anything that gets
in its way.

Tiger Shark

Here are some things
that have been found
inside tiger sharks!

Not all sharks are dangerous
to people.
This big shark has very small teeth.
It eats tiny sea plants and animals.

Basking Shark

Most sharks are fast swimmers.
Some can swim as fast
as a motorboat.

Mako Shark

Other sharks are not fast at all.
This shark mostly rests
on the ocean floor.